Rookie
Read-About®
Science

How Things Work:
Fire Trucks

by Joanne Mattern

Content Consultant

Nanci R. Vargus, Ed.D.
Professor Emeritus, University of Indianapolis

Reading Consultant

Jeanne M. Clidas, Ph.D.
Reading Specialist

Children's Press®
An Imprint of Scholastic Inc.

A CIP catalog record of this book is available from the Library of Congress.
ISBN 978-0-531-21373-5 (library binding) – ISBN 978-0-531-21461-9 (pbk.)

Produced by Spooky Cheetah Press
Design by Keith Plechaty

Printed in China 62

SCHOLASTIC, CHILDREN'S PRESS, ROOKIE READ-ABOUT®, and associated logos are trademarks and/or registered trademarks of Scholastic Inc.

1 2 3 4 5 6 7 8 9 10 R 25 24 23 22 21 20 19 18 17 16

Photographs©: cover: Christophe Testi/Alamy Images; 3 top left: Jiri Vaclavek/Shutterstock, Inc.; 3 top right: scenery2/Shutterstock, Inc.; 3 bottom: Nerthuz/Shutterstock, Inc.; 4: Andreas Keuchel/Alamy Images; 7: Daniel Bockwoldt/EPA/Newscom; 8: Tracey Whitefoot/Alamy Images; 12: Christian Oth/Getty Images Assignment for Scholastic; 15: Darren Greenwood/Media Bakery; 16: Transtock/Superstock, Inc.; 19: Suzanne Tucker/Shutterstock, Inc.; 20: Ingram Publishing/Newscom; 23: VanderWolf Images/Shutterstock, Inc.; 24: Hot Shots/Alamy Images; 26-27 background: Keith Plechaty; 26-27 center: Malcolm Leman/Shutterstock, Inc.; 26 top: Ed Endicott/Alamy Images; 26 bottom: Everett Collection/Superstock, Inc.; 27 top: Le Do/Shutterstock, Inc.; 27 bottom: E-One; 30: Morita Holdings Corporation; 31 top: Monty Rakusen/Media Bakery; 31 center top: Tracey Whitefoot/Alamy Images; 31 center bottom: Hot Shots/Alamy Images; 31 bottom: Ed Endicott/Alamy Images.

Illustrations by Jeffrey Chandler/Art Gecko Studios!

Table of Contents

Fire Truck to the Rescue!

Whooo! Whooo! Firefighters race along in their fire truck. The truck is more than a way to get somewhere, though. It is a firefighting machine!

There are two kinds of fire trucks.
A **pumper truck** carries water.

A firefighter sprays water from the tank of a pumper truck.

A ladder is folded up on top of the truck when not in use.

A **ladder truck** is another kind of fire truck. Most ladder trucks do not carry water. They carry ladders! Most ladders go up 100 feet (30 meters). They can reach to the top of a five-story building.

FUN FACT!

Ladders on some New York City fire trucks are super tall. They can reach to the top of a 15-story building.

How a Pumper Truck Works

A pumper truck can hold more than 1,000 gallons of water. That is enough to fill about 20 bathtubs!

Firefighters attach hoses to the truck. Then they turn on a pump. That forces the water through the hoses and onto the fire.

10

Parts of a Pumper Truck

This drawing shows the inside of the back of the truck. The tank of water is here.

Firefighters spray water from this gun onto the fire.

This is where the hoses connect to the truck.

This is the pump that forces the water through the hoses.

A lot of water sprays through a large hose. That makes it hard to control. One firefighter cannot do it alone.

A large hose sprays a lot of water at once. Firefighters would use it on a big fire. A smaller hose sprays less water. Firefighters would use it on a smaller fire.

How a Ladder Truck Works

Sometimes there is a fire near the top of a tall building. That is a job for a ladder truck.

The ladder lies flat on top of the truck. At the fire, a firefighter presses a button on the truck. A pump lifts the ladder up.

FUN FACT!

The ladder on a fire truck cannot reach the top of a skyscraper. Instead, firefighters go inside the building and climb up the stairs. They attach their hoses to pipes inside the building.

Most ladder trucks do not carry water. Firefighters attach their hoses to a fire hydrant on the street. A fire hydrant is connected to water under the ground.

fire hydrant

Inside the Firefighting Machine

Some trucks carry up to eight firefighters. The driver and the captain sit in the front seats. Everyone else sits behind them. There is a button on the **dashboard** to turn on the siren.

Fire trucks also carry a lot of tools. They carry **nozzles** to attach to the different hoses.

They carry chopping tools, like axes. Firefighters use them to break down doors and to break through windows. That helps them reach the fire inside.

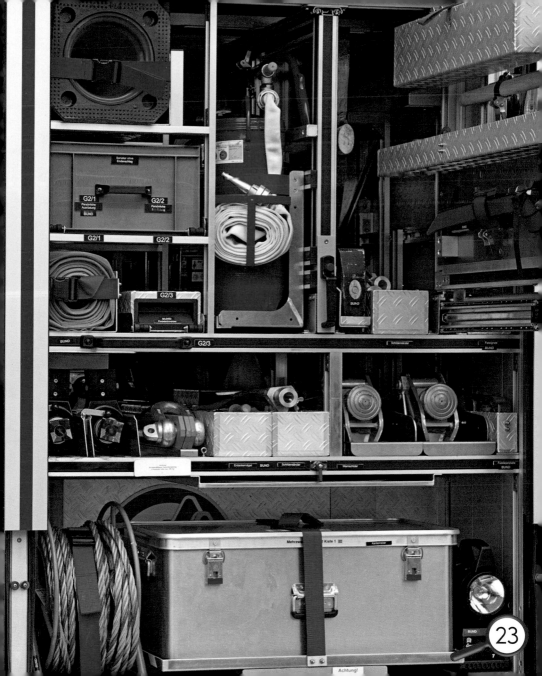

Fire trucks also carry first-aid supplies. Firefighters use them to help people who are hurt.

Now you know how a fire truck works. It has everything a firefighter needs!

Timeline

Motorized Pumper Truck

1958

1900

1950

1890

Horse-Drawn Fire Truck

26

Modern
Fire Truck

1990s

2000

2010

CR 137 LADDER

137 TALLEST AERIAL LADDER

Tallest Fire Truck in North America

Super Science

Ask an adult for help. Do not attempt this science experiment on your own!

The pumps on a pumper truck use air to force water out of a hose and onto a fire. This experiment will show you how a water pump works. (This experiment will get messy! It is best to do it in a sink or bathtub, or outside.)

You Will Need: Empty plastic water bottle, pen or small scissors, straw, adhesive putty, water, balloon

1. Use the pen or scissors to poke a small hole about ⅓ of the way from the bottom of the bottle.

2. Push the straw into the bottle so one end is sticking out and up from the hole. Use putty to keep the straw in place.

3.

Pour water into the bottle so it covers the hole and the straw and fills the bottle halfway. Plug any leaks with more putty.

Notice that no water flows out of the straw. That is because nothing is pushing the water out of the bottle.

4.

Blow up the balloon. Pinch the neck of the balloon closed and stretch the lip around the mouth of the bottle.

5.

Let go of the balloon. What happens? Water flows out of the straw.

Why This Works:

As with the pump on a fire truck, air from the balloon pushes against the water in the bottle and pumps the water out through the straw.

That's Amazing!

Could this be the future of firefighting?

Fighting a fire in the forest is different from fighting a fire in a city or town. Some forest fires are far from roads, so fire trucks cannot get to them. It can be hard for firefighters to communicate with one another. And there are no fire hydrants. It is hard to get water to put out a fire!

But a new fire truck called Morita's Wildfire Truck (above) may solve these problems. The Wildfire truck can drive on rough, rocky ground. So it is able to reach forest fires. It also has a communications system inside. People in the truck can talk to firefighters in other locations. That helps them put out the fire faster. And the Wildfire truck does not need much water. It uses a chemical foam that does not hurt the environment to put out the fire.

Glossary

dashboard (DASH-bord): instrument panel in a fire truck where siren control is located

ladder truck (LAD-ur TRUK): fire truck with a tall ladder on top

nozzles (NAHZ-uhls): spouts that direct the flow of liquid from the end of a hose

pumper truck (PUHM-per TRUK): fire truck that carries water inside

Index

Facts for Now

Visit this Scholastic Web site for more information on fire trucks:
www.factsfornow.scholastic.com
Enter the keywords **Fire Trucks**

About the Author

Joanne Mattern is the author of many nonfiction books for children. Science is one of her favorite subjects to write about! She lives in New York State with her husband, four children, and numerous pets.